Colin Oates Judo
Getting Started

Colin Oates

Howard Oates

Oakamoor
Publishing

Published in 2015 by Oakamoor Publishing, an imprint of Bennion Kearny Limited.

ISBN: 978-1-910773-08-6

Published by Oakamoor Publishing, Bennion Kearny Limited
6 Woodside
Churnet View Road
Oakamoor
Staffordshire
ST10 3AE

www.BennionKearny.com

Colin Oates

I started judo at the age of five, so it is true to say I cannot remember a time when the sport was not a part of my life. As part of a judo family I was able to practice at home with my brother David and sisters Charlotte and Vicky and whilst growing up I was never short of training partners!

My father and co-author of this book, Howard, has been my personal coach since my career began and has travelled across the world with me attending competitions and training camps. In that time, I have represented Great Britain at Olympic, World, and European Championships and in 2014 won the Commonwealth Games gold medal for England.

I have been crowned British Champion on eight occasions as a youth and senior player and my father collected four British Veterans Championships in the 90s. In addition, I have won European and Grand Slam medals on the International Circuit.

This book sets out to introduce the newer player to the sport in a gentle form by demonstrating that judo can be practiced without the need for continuous heavy impacts. Learning techniques in clusters, in a drill-like regime, is a somewhat unique but tried-and-tested formula which enables players of all ages to remember a variety of techniques.

Although I choose to fight around the world, this book will show how judo is very much a family sport. The various demonstrations in the photographs are performed by my sisters and longstanding training partner, David. Even my young nephew, Reece, assisted by performing breakfalls. If ever a sport can be shared by a family it is the sport of Judo.

Finally a thank you to my mother Denise who has organised and arranged many a judo trip overseas and in Britain, and endured many an early start to travel to far off places so we could fight all over the world.

Colin

Table of Contents

What is Judo

The word *Judo* translates into the "gentle art". Anyone who has ever engaged in a Judo contest would almost certainly disagree with this view! Whilst it is true that there are no punches or kicks, and there is no intention to display a violent demeanour, truly gentle is something of an understatement. The strength and commitment to fitness involved in contest Judo is phenomenal.

Judo emanates from Japan where Jigoro Kano, in simple terms, during the 19th century removed the dangerous bits from *jiu jitsu* and in effect created a martial art that was safe to perform in a competitive manner. Since then, it has evolved into an Olympic sport.

There have been countless manuals that have covered the complete history of Judo development. We are not seeking to cover the same ground but it is worth mentioning that, in recent years, Judo as an international sport has matured to a point where there are now worldwide prize money tournaments, as well as a transparent international circuit where players can enter events and see themselves climb on national, European, and world ranking lists.

The sport has also figured in the Olympics since 1964 (only being dropped for one games in 1968) and unlike many other martial arts, and other combat sports, we have an only one recognised world championship which is run by the International Judo Federation (the internationally recognised governing body for Judo). This championship is run annually apart from during an Olympic year. Judo's governing body runs Olympic qualification events in many countries in conjunction with national governing bodies.

The International Judo Federation has continued to find ways to improve the look of the sport in a bid to make it more dynamic and more attractive to a wider audience. The abolition of leg grabs from contest Judo and limiting the time spent in groundwork can be said, arguably, to have gone some way towards making the sport more audience friendly. The introduction of one player wearing a blue suit and one a white suit has, in turn, made it easier for the public to identify who is who in a contest.

Many people like the changes, and many do not, but a great leap forward is the introduction of video technology at major events where officials can review scoring situations and overrule and correct what are considered to be incorrect scores, or scores that may otherwise have been overlooked completely. This has taken the sport into the 21st century and has made scoring much more consistent.

There is, however, a view that the sport's somewhat confusing scoring system could be simplified. Again, various recent rule changes eliminating the lowest scoring throw the *koka* (3 point score) may have made some improvement but even the most experienced referee would admit that trying to explain the rules and scoring system to a person for the first time is problematic to say the least!

Fortunately, for the purposes of this book, there is no need to perform a detailed study into the contest rules of Judo but more to the point just as Judo has continued to develop so too has the mixed martial art circuit and this is both as helpful as it may be possibly destructive. Many Judo clubs seek to increase their membership numbers by attracting players whose interests are not primarily in the sport of Judo but are looking to improve their skills of ground fighting which is a major side of MMA (or what is also known as cage fighting). Some clubs even engage in bare top grappling, which is more closely aligned to cage fighting situations. The emergence of the MMA circuit cannot be ignored and it is possible that, eventually, there will be more Judo clubs that cater for players who want to improve their grappling for the purpose of cage fighting. There is a growing professional circuit and big MMA contests are now promoted in Las Vegas on a par with the boxing.

It is also true to highlight the crossover with jiu jitsu, particularly Brazilian jiu jitsu, where there is a great emphasis on groundwork. Certainly in some countries the national governing bodies control the administration of both Judo and jiu jitsu.

No doubt, Judo will continue to evolve. We are very fortunate to be an Olympic sport - a fact that sets Judo aside from other strains of martial arts. Whilst Judo remains in the most prestigious games competition in the world it will retain its unique identity. However, it falls to the sport's governing body - the International Judo Federation - to remain vigilant to change and ensure that our sport remains true to its core spirit, namely, inflicting defeat upon an opponent without physical damage to the person. This is not to say there is no place for martial arts clubs that cater for the MMA side to things; they too serve their function and cater for the needs of many who wish to study and engage in that side of combat sport.

An insight into getting started as a player

Taking up Judo can be a daunting prospect whether you are a youngster, an adult looking to start the sport at a mature age, or a parent searching for the best club to coach your children. There are many different considerations relating to personal needs when looking to get involved but one important aspect that is of paramount importance is ensuring the club you attend is attached to a governing body and the coach or coaches are fully qualified. With the internet, it is a little easier to research information but remain aware of situations where coaches try to sell their clubs by 'elaborating' on their past achievements. Often just following local press reports will yield valuable information on the quality of your local club and its coaching standards. There are now many global websites that carry worldwide Judo results and information and, together with the many Judo forums online, it pays to do thorough research especially when looking for junior clubs.

Although Judo is a fighting sport it may seem strange to learn there are many clubs that consider themselves non-competitive just as some boast they *are* competitive. Of course, the wonderful selling point with Judo - that pleases many a parent - is that Judo is one of the few fighting sports where the intention is to defeat without inflicting injury on the opponent.

As a parent looking to find a club for a junior player, it is likely your son or daughter is looking to take up Judo because it is a sport where advancement can be easily measured by grading exams; players are awarded different coloured belts that relate to their ability levels. Most junior sessions will happily cater for players just looking for belts as well as those children with aspirations of taking part in competitions. It is a little more complex for adults taking up the sport a little later in life and care should be taken to find a club that does not place too great an emphasis on competitive Judo. The majority of adults need to earn a living and clubs that undertake serious competitive Judo will tend to do a great deal of *randori* (sparring) and this is where - with a relatively inexperienced adult - there is the possibility of injury (especially in the early stages).

Most clubs will let you wear jogging bottoms and lend you or your children a jacket in the early weeks and it is wise to allow a few weeks to pass before investing in the full gear called a *Judogi* (Judo suit). Once you or your children are committed, it is vital you take out a licence from the governing body, which provides insurance cover and will allow participation in competitions and gradings.

The inside of a *dojo* (a place where martial arts get taught) can seem intimidating at first. However, it will not take very long to mix in with a bunch of good-natured people. One dojo will always be different to another with regards to atmosphere and etiquette, and it is good to remember that if one style of coaching does not appeal to you there are always other clubs. There are many different styles and approaches from one coach to another. The two words the beginner must learn quickly are *hajime* (start) and *matte* (stop).

Contest Judo

We have already covered the fact that some clubs will claim to be competitive and others non-competitive. The reality, however, is that sport is competitive in the sense that players want to win or become the best they can be.

In Judo, there is a belt colour structure that denotes your ability and experience and it is this very special aspect to martial arts that attracts most players into a dojo. It varies from association to association and from country to country but the ultimate aim is to become a black belt, which indicates a skilful player. But does skilful also mean an accomplished fighter as well?

There are many different grading schemes worldwide. Some involve having to fight other players at grading examinations as well as doing theory; other schemes involve theory only. There are some countries where the awarding of a belt is at the sole discretion of the senior coach. Whatever the scheme, though, somehow they generally level out and get the same result in the end. The majority of black belts in Judo are formidable opponents in combat.

Most individuals who take up the sport will not find competitive Judo very inviting. Without doubt, it is hard and without a professional circuit where large amounts of money can be made - there are good reasons to avoid it.

In most countries, there are 'novice only' tournaments which limit the belt grade of the entry (i.e. orange or perhaps yellow belt and under). Because adult novices who wish to compete are at a premium, tournaments are unlikely to attract large numbers of entrants so although they may be weight-banded it is likely that groups will have to be merged. In real terms, this puts the smaller player at greater risk as they give away excess weight. Of course, it may be to a player's advantage if they are bigger than the opponent before them, but generally it is a situation where the novice adult needs protection. It is better to decline the offer to fight much heavier players than risk injury; a proactive coach who cares should monitor the groups their players find themselves in.

When entering adult competitions there are many other considerations. Most countries have some form of ranking system (usually based on competition results) and competitions that carry ranking points of any sort should be avoided by all but serious players. With the growth of centralised training centres in many countries, even your better club black belt players are probably wasting their time and their entry fee as the likelihood will be that the ranking events will be flooded by serious players. Many of these players will be in full time training and club players - training twice a week and working, say, in an office environment - will not usually be any match for the full time career player.

In some European countries, there are Judo leagues and, like soccer, you can find your level and enjoy your sport competing against players of equal ability. This is an excellent way of introducing adults into contest Judo as it combines a social and team spirit similar to many other team sports. Such leagues work very efficiently in countries like Belgium where there is a high density of clubs in a relatively small area. Not all countries are blessed with a high number of clubs and players and this is sad because the national league days in Belgium are very special and we, as a family, have been honoured to be associated with the leagues for many years.

Guiding younger players into competition is very much easier. For a start, there are many more of them and children are much more competitive than adults tend to be as they have less fear of injury. However, caution needs to be exercised, as it is easy to lose young players from the sport by pushing them into competition (the same can also be said for early *randori*). Sometimes, parents with high expectations inadvertently put too much pressure on their children; no one wants to disappoint Mum and Dad. Also, bear in mind that many countries have minimum age limits for children competing in tournaments. The British Judo Association forbids players younger than eight from competing for medals.

There are many types of Judo competition formats. In addition to the more accepted style where two players start standing and try to throw, hold, strangle or armlock to victory you can find competitions that start on the ground where standing Judo is not allowed. These *newaza* tournaments are a great way of introducing players young and old into Judo competition where the impact of a hard landing is removed. Adult newaza tournaments are more varied than junior ones as adults have the full range of techniques at their disposal (e.g. strangles). Junior events can be a little laborious as Judoka can only pin each other.

The competition format can vary considerably from a straight knockout to pools of players all fighting each other. In some knockout situations, you are guaranteed a second contest even if you lose the first whilst in other systems you must lose to a losing semi-finalist to be brought back to fight toward the bronze medal stage. In some parts of the USA, there is only one bronze medal whilst in Europe there always seems to be two bronze medals. The format is at the discretion of the governing body and the Competition Controller.

In addition, there are Kata competitions where players perform a set style of movements for a group of judges. Whilst the *uke* generally suffers a fair bit of impact it is all rehearsed so many players prefer this mode of competition, which is also a wonderful learning aid. The katas form a major part of grading syllabuses in many countries so they need to be learnt if you want to climb the belt ladder.

Getting Hands On!

Breakfalls

The skill involved in perfecting the breakfall should not be underestimated. If a player has little fear of being thrown it is likely they will be less inhibited in their Judo. Few players truly enjoy the prospect of being thrown but a player who has no confidence in landing safely will find improvement of their throwing ability restricted, as they are less likely to commit a 100 per cent to a throw.

The basic fall should be performed from a low position as illustrated below. From this height, there is little chance of damage even to the most clumsy of novices. The most important thing is to keep the chin tucked in and the arm breaking the fall outstretched to ensure no damage to the head or the elbows. It is vital to perform the breakfall on both sides.

[1] Breakfalls should be practised from this low position to reduce impact with your head tucked into your chin.

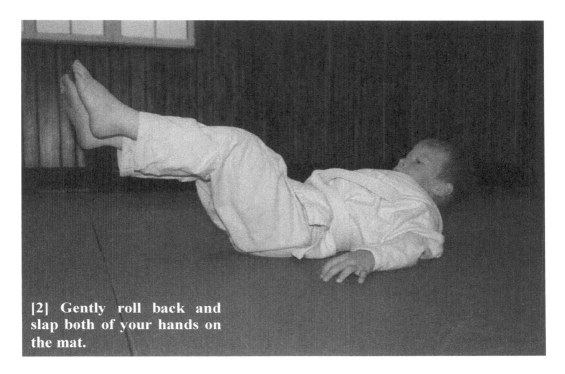

[2] Gently roll back and slap both of your hands on the mat.

Injuries often occur from players clashing heads as they attempt to breakfall without checking the clearance behind themselves. So look behind you!

The next two pictures demonstrate the forward breakfall we describe as "The Superman" simply because it appears you are about to fly off into the sky. There is a degree of impact on the elbows but it is still better than crashing one's face into the mat!

[3] The same posture is relevant for the next breakfall.

[4] Gently lurch forward onto your forearms.

Another type of breakfall practice is to work with a partner who will remove your means of support forcing you to roll onto your back. A partner can pull your

10

furthest arm and nearest leg gently or with force to speed up the turn as required. In this way, a player is able to affect a heavy breakfall with their free arm but from a low level thus reducing the possibility of injury in the early days of a Judo career.

[5] Take hold of the furthest arm and closest leg.

[6] Pull hard on the arm and leg and drive forward with your body.

[7] The player being turned is able to slap the mat with their free hand and affect a safe breakfall again from a low level reducing any heavy impact.

In the next section, a programme of movements will be outlined with a heavy focus on balance and direction. The throwing motions could be described as some type of *Kata* (a stylised set of techniques performed in a very regimented manner). Traditional katas are somewhat out of date with modern competition Judo rules which, at present, prevent any hand movements below the belt. Indeed, modern Judo rules, laid down by the governing body (the International Judo Federation) have made the sport far more dynamic to watch but has created headaches for Judo coaches who have had many techniques removed from the competitive Judo circuit.

Katas that are still required by most governing bodies for grading purposes.

- *Nage No Kata.* A series of throws on the left and right side.
- *Katame No Kata.* A series of groundwork moves involving hold downs, strangles, and armlocks.

There are several other Katas, but the ones above are the more common and figure in most Judo associations' grading structures.

An insight into directional Judo

Trying to remember the various techniques is not easy, especially in contest situations where reactions will be quicker than thought. Learning techniques in cluster movements may help a player to react effectively rather than waste a split second thinking of 'how' to react. The concept of directional Judo is based on traditional katas but should not be considered one. Working on one's technique is simply an educational tool.

1. Breaking balance
2. Throwing in the same direction as your partner or opponent is moving
3. Providing the player with a throw on four sides

Diagram one (below) best describes the theory of pattern Judo. It is not so easy to practise on a smaller mat with larger numbers.

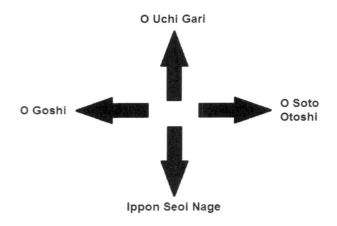

The theory of pattern Judo

The throws in the pattern can be performed in any order as the main purpose of the exercise is to throw in the direction your partner is moving but it is probably best to start with *O Soto Otoshi* which is easy to teach both in technique, balance and direction. Now before we describe the basic element of simply taking hold of your opponent or partner, an explanation is required.

French Judo has for many years been outstanding and France has produced many great players. The turning point in our thinking on both training and coaching stemmed back to the British Open (one of the last to be held at Crystal Palace back in 2003). We observed that many of the French players were left-handed in stance. So many that it did not seem to be by chance but rather a deliberate policy.

It was clear that this was no coincidence and we monitored French players thereafter, as well as other world elite players, and discovered that a very high percentage were left-handed stance players. As such, we started to coach all novices with a left-handed stance.

Assuming the majority of Judo players are right-handed, the wrong way left-handed stance, it seems, might just give a player a head start in attacking the left side of an opponent and in addition will make it awkward for one's opponent to grip. Beginning Judo as a left-handed player does not cause too many problems to a person who is naturally right-handed. It is true there will be a yearning to switch to the right-handed side of the opponent but it will not take too long for a new Judo player to adjust.

So, it will come as no surprise that *[8]* and *[9]* demonstrate a typical left-handed grip to begin the pattern of throws (one of a great many varieties of grip). It must,

14

at this stage, be emphasised that gripping is a subject matter in itself and the grips in this publication will be basic sleeve/lapel.

[8] Regardless of which side you grip - ensure it is a firm one.

[9] This style of grip is regarded as traditional Japanese but there are many variations.

Cluster One

O Soto O Toshi (Major Outer Drop)

Start the movement as *tori* (the person performing the technique) with a left-handed grip (i.e. left hand on opponent's right lapel and right hand on your opponent's left sleeve just under their elbow). Pull first with your right hand to the right placing *uke* (your opponent) on their left foot, pull back uke so they are standing on their right foot, then pull hard with your right hand and place your left leg behind uke's left leg…

[10] O Soto Otoshi – part I.

…then pull hard with your right hand with the intention of placing uke's head at your right leg.

[11] O Soto Otoshi- part II. When throwing your partner in practice always help brace their fall by holding their lapel tightly and guiding them to the ground.

Completing the throw is optional as, often, it is possible to complete the whole pattern without throwing - just pulling to the point of the throw (but without the necessity of subjecting your uke to constant mat impact).

O Uchi Gari (Major Inner Reap)

The second throw in the pattern is *O Uchi Gari*

With this technique, we have found that it helps if *tori* (the person performing the throw) hops on their right leg and retains the same grip as O Soto Otoshi (right hand on the sleeve and left hand gripping just under uke's left elbow).

Uke should move backwards allowing tori to hop forward and hook uke's right leg with tori's left leg. Take note that in hooking uke's leg it sometimes helps if you can pin uke's leg to your own thigh to prevent them stepping out. Again, it must be said that this throw can be performed in a number of ways and this method emphasises directional movement as a basis for later perfection.

[12] O Uchi Gari - part I. Ensure you use your leg to grasp at your opponent's leg sufficiently high enough to prevent them stepping off the throw.

[13] O Uchi Gari - part II. The sleeve and the lapel grips should be firm as you enter side-on into your opponent.

Ippon Seoi Nage (Shoulder Throw)

The third movement in the pattern is *Ippon Seoi Nage* - one of the most popular and dynamic throws in Judo. Often portrayed in many a TV series or movie there are several variations with this technique. There are whole books just dedicated to this one throw!

In these circumstances, it is assumed that we are learning the throw for the first time and there are a number of matters the novice should consider when studying this throw. The throw that offers the least damage to the throwing person is the standing variety but this means your partner is being thrown from a considerable height and this can put you off as a novice on the wrong end of the throw. You could drop onto one or both knees to perform the throw, and whilst gentler on the partner (as they will fall from a lower height) it can cause damage to your knees over the long term. The International Judo Federation's current rules forbid attacks involving grabbing legs and, as a result, there has been a rise in the use of this type of technique. So, there is a need to be proficient in throws such as this.

Let's take a look at Ippon Seoi Nage.

Start with a left-handed grip, with tori's left hand firmly holding uke's lapel and tori's right hand gripping uke's left sleeve. The design here is to retain a left-handed grip whilst performing a right-handed technique.

[14] Uke is on the left, Tori is on the right. The sleeve grip is the more common entry grip but it is possible to grip uke's lapel instead and surprise your opponent by attacking off the lapel side.

As tori turns into uke's right hand, tori retains the lapel grip whilst moving his right hand under uke's left arm

[15] Most players drive their incoming arm upward but you can also grip uke's sleeve with your right hand too.

[16] From this position if you lift your heels and move onto a tiptoe position you will create an extra spring that lifts your opponent upwards.

As tori's right arm aims to get under uke's left arm, tori's right leg steps across uke's body and tori turns their body into uke. Tori then drives their right arm upward. At no time does tori release their lapel grip.

This attack should take an unsuspecting opponent by surprise as it is a right-handed attack off a left-handed grip which should cause some level of confusion. The more mature player can collapse to the right knee and the elite player will almost certainly drop to both knees.

[17] The classic one knee drop certainly is more knee friendly as Colin clasps his opponent's arm with both hands for extra control.

[18] This entry, when performed at speed, requires a speedy attack (perhaps best described as a leap into the throw).

The inclusion of Ippon Seoi Nage in the pattern is to attack an opponent who is walking onto you. This fits nicely as we now have a throw when someone is moving to our right (O Soto O Toshi), a throw on an opponent moving backwards (O Uchi Gari), and now an attack when someone is moving towards us. This will provide the beginner with the concept of throwing an opponent in the direction that they are moving. As mentioned, Judo is often described as the gentle art. Exponents of the sport will tell you it is better to use someone's momentum against them rather than meet it head on. With this set of throws, the novice should have a better idea of how to use the direction a player moves to your advantage.

Providing a throw to the left (as you face an opponent) can prove somewhat problematic as you need to revert to a right-handed grip (i.e. right hand on the lapel and left hand on the opponent's right sleeve; note that the right hand does not, in this instance, take a sleeve but rather slips behind the partner's back and grabs the belt). In real terms, pure *O Goshi* (Hip Throw) is a throw involving a deep entry, with your hip, into your opponent's body - with a firm grip behind your opponent's back (gripping either the belt or just above). The deeper the entry the easier the throw becomes. Indeed, it is possible for a lightweight to walk around the mat with a much heavier opponent sitting on their hip if the entry is correct and deep. It is perhaps best described, visually, in *[19]* and *[20]*.

[19] In turning into your opponent there must be no gap between your body and that of the opponent.

[20] Whilst grabbing the belt is more secure, a grip of the jacket will suffice and still give sufficient control to land your opponent safely.

When performing O Goshi, it is optional whether you grip the belt or grip the back of the Judo suit.

The pattern movement is now complete and if performed without completing the throw is ideal for the novice (especially the older player who has no intention of qualifying for the Olympic Games). Often, younger players competing for the first time will attempt throws that stand very little chance of success because their opponent is moving in the wrong direction.

Cluster Two

Tai O Toshi (Body Drop)

Next, we look at *Tai O Toshi*. With this attack, it is vital to coordinate hand and foot. Taking a left hand grip on the right lapel of your opponent's jacket, and with your right hand grip their left sleeve, step sharply between their feet with your left leg. Simultaneously move your left elbow into your opponent's left armpit

[21] As Tori steps in, there is a need to begin the turn into your opponent's body (to avoid the potential of your outstretched left foot being swept away).

Turning your back into your opponent, you should also swing your right leg back.

Then place your left leg past your opponent ensuring your left foot is on tiptoe. If your heel is on the mat, the throw may still work but you should aim to have flexibility in your knee which should be pointing downward.

The final stage of the throw is to turn your head away from your opponent.

[24] Turning your head away from your opponent may seem like a small detail but will make a significant difference.

In the early stages of practice try to resist fully completing the throw especially if your opponent/partner is (like you) a novice. The objective is to develop a variety of techniques that link and if your opponent/partner is still on their feet it is possible to move smoothly to the next throw in the sequence.

With the same left-handed grip on your opponent's jacket, it is possible to effect *O Soto Maki Komi (Outer Winding Throw)*. This technique is performed down the opponent's other wing (the right side of the opponent just like *Ippon Seoi Nage*). In fact, there are some similarities between the two throws. In Ippon Seoi Nage, your right hand went under the opponent's right arm but in O Soto Maki Komi, your right arm goes over the top.

[25] The bigger the step with your right leg the more likely this throw will be a winner.

As your right arm moves, you should take a huge step with your right leg

[26] A competition player determined on obtaining victory will wrap up the opponent's right arm whereas the novice would be well-advised to use their right hand to assist their landing.

The bigger the step the less likely your opponent will retain their balance so if you are keen on moving onto the third throw in the cluster try not to overstep. A word of warning before moving to the third throw in the sequence, this technique is a heavy one and involves both players collapsing to the mat if executed to a conclusion. It is advisable for the person doing the throw to breakfall on the arm that has been thrown over the opponent's right arm rather than grabbing their right arm. In reality, it is a certainty the thrower will land on the person being thrown so the thrower's fall is cushioned by their opponent. This is an unforgiving throw popular with heavyweights who use their bodyweight to drag down their opponents. Nonetheless, it can be used equally effectively by lighter players.

[27] This is the ideal drill for this technique. To execute a conclusion to this throw, tori only needs to dive forward onto the mat.

Assuming you are keen to complete the third throw in the cluster, and have left your opponent upright, keep your left hand exactly where it started in the first throw of this second cluster. The left hand will have remained in the same place throughout the movement. From this grip, it is possible to go back to a left hand throw of *Uchi Mata (Inner Thigh)*. Ideally, the grip should be deeper (possibly stretching behind the opponent's neck) however, the objective of developing throws in clusters is to offer variety from a lapel grip that remains in place throughout the sequence. In any event, the Russian Squad was using the lower lapel grip with this throw to disguise the attack with great effect some years ago.

Your right arm should assume control of your opponent's left sleeve ready for a turn into their body. The Judo purist, aiming to achieve perfect footwork, would step with their left foot to a point just in front of the opponent's left foot and bring their right leg back to just in front of the opponent's right foot.

[28] When drilling this throw, many players start a considerable distance from the opponent / training partner so they can swing in and gain momentum.

[29] The aim is to place both of your feet on the inside of your opponent's. However, the throw can still be successful if your right foot is on the outside of your opponent's right foot.

At this point, both players will be facing the same direction. The foot positions may not be exact but from this position, your opponent is vulnerable to being thrown.

Pull hard with your right arm whilst driving your left arm across their body and, at the same time, lift your left leg between the legs of your opponent.

[30] The perfect entry.

[31] The launch can now be commenced for what is possibly the most beautiful throw in judo.

This form of execution is open to criticism. In Japan, it is likely there would be an emphasis on lifting your opponent onto their toes before turning your back as this breaks balance and lessens the risk of being countered with a throw. It is also possible to drive your left leg into the opponent's right leg effectively smashing it off the floor and into the air, thus placing your opponent on one standing leg. If an attack is successful, it probably matters not what variations occur in the movement.

On completing this second cluster you have seven throws in your armoury: six throws with a left hand grip (two of which throw in the opposite direction: *Ippon Seoi Nage* and *O Soto Maki Komi*) to what an opponent would be expecting.

In cluster 2, your partner can remain still while you practice your footwork and grips unlike the first cluster. However, it is vital to perform all standing techniques on the move, as this will stimulate a realistic contest situation.

In turning to the next cluster, it may seem strange but to perform this section we are dependent on our partner performing badly as they need to demonstrate weak and poor technique.

Cluster Three

This cluster will give the novice an understanding of how to counterattack a player. In using the techniques already covered, the novice will also learn the pitfalls of getting it wrong and not committing sufficiently to the throw. It is usually the latter that fails the player.

We will look at three counterattacks.

1. *O Soto O Toshi* countered with *O Soto O Toshi*.
2. *Tai O Toshi* countered with *Tani O Toshi*.
3. *Uchi Mata* countered with *Ura Nage*.

Before embarking on counterattacks - a word of warning for the novice: *they only work if the opponent's initial attack fails*. In a nutshell, you should not wait to be attacked in the hope and belief that you are capable of throwing an opponent with a counter. It is best practice to attack. To counterattack in Judo is like a soccer team trying to absorb pressure from the opposing team and not having possession of the ball yet believing they will score on the break from defence. It is a recipe for disaster in both sports.

Counter 1: O Soto O Toshi with O Soto O Toshi

If the opponent fails to break your balance or lacks commitment in the pull of your sleeve, simply pull hard on their left sleeve and drive them to the floor.

[32] A weak attack, or a stretched one.

[33] The attacker suddenly becomes the attacked.

For the purposes of this cluster it is necessary to throw but, as always, show concern in practice for your partner/opponent on the mat. With this technique you are learning a counterattack without the need to learn a new throw but it is possible to make one slight variation on the counter that actually introduces a new technique *O Soto Gari* (Major Outer Reap). This is probably more effective.

As your opponent steps past you, simply lift their leg with yours effectively reaping it away.

[34] Just lifting your left leg changes the name of the throw and is probably a more effective way of dealing with this mode of attack.

Counter 2: Tai O Toshi with Tani O Toshi (Valley Drop)

Without deterring the novice from specialising in Tai O Toshi it is fair to say this is probably one of the easiest throws in the syllabus to counter. There are many ways to avoid being thrown with this technique even if it is performed well by your opponent.

The initial entry into Tai O Toshi in placing your left (or right leg if right-handed) forward will leave a player prone to foot sweeps or at best prone to an attack on the outstretched leg. The counter to be used for the purpose of this cluster has been selected as it introduces what is described as a sacrificial throw. So described because it involves a player sacrificing their standing posture and throwing themselves to the ground.

[35] The classic attack of Tai O Toshi perhaps performed in a weak manner.

As your opponent turns in, simply step over their outstretched leg with your right leg and straighten it behind both of their legs; in essence sit down whilst retaining your grip of their sleeve and lapel.

[36] I have time to step over the attacker's leg.

[37] From this position, I stretch my leg further and could easily complete the throw by sitting down.

This would not in general involve a high scoring throw, as considerable force would be needed to place the opponent flat on their back. Although this throw is usually described as a counterattack, it can be used in an offensive manner too. The problem with any sacrificial move, however, is that in relinquishing your standing posture there is always considerable uncertainty as to the position you may land in. The result may be underneath an opponent and even though they may not have scored a throw against you, it is inevitable you will be fighting a rear-guard action to get back on your feet, which can be tiring. So, extreme caution is always required when utilising sacrificial throws of which there are many.

Counter 3: Uchi Mata with Ura Nage (Rear Throw)

This counterattack can only be described as a beast of a throw and should be practised with a crashmat (most clubs have extra cushioned mats fit for such purpose).

As your opponent steps in with their Uchi Mata, bend your knees so that your right knee in particular lifts the opponent's left thigh, placing your right arm on their back and gripping whatever you can of the jacket. Fling yourself backwards and, whilst falling, turn into your opponent ensuring they land on their back and you land on your side

[38] I anticipate a big hip throw from my attacking brother.

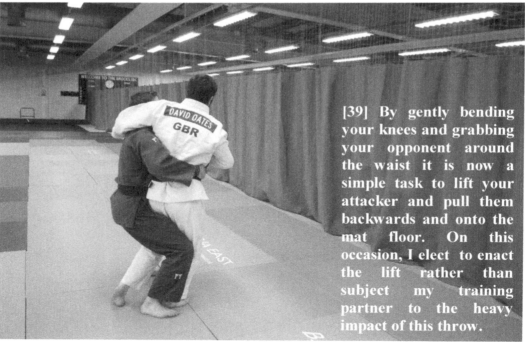

[39] By gently bending your knees and grabbing your opponent around the waist it is now a simple task to lift your attacker and pull them backwards and onto the mat floor. On this occasion, I elect to enact the lift rather than subject my training partner to the heavy impact of this throw.

The use of a crashmat is not just in the interest of your partner but also for your protection too. In truth, it is unlikely this throw is commonly used in dojos and certainly the more responsible player would not apply this technique very often. The throw is a legal one and it should stand as a reminder to players to ensure their initial attack is committed and as technically correct as possible to avoid this counter.

In practicing this set of throws, it is vital you have a partner who is willing to cooperate with you - otherwise improvement becomes impossible. Also, bear in mind that most of the throws are from the left-handed grip and it is more common for an opponent to be right-handed so a very willing training partner is required, one who is prepared to adapt grips and stance so that you can adjust your footwork and grips as necessary. Many instruction manuals will be specific on gripping and footwork but in the final analysis it is 'what works for you' given your unique physical attributes. This is not easy and requires many hours of drills.

Combination Techniques

Cluster Four

The next cluster of throws introduces the concept of combination techniques. The question (to which there is no definitive answer) is whether a player should attack with one technique and turn it into another on purpose? Or should sufficient force be put into the initial first attack to render the second throw unnecessary? Many coaches will argue that if the first attack is executed well enough there is no need to think of an alternative as it should have thrown your opponent. There is also an argument that it is a part of tactical Judo to set an opponent up for the second planned throw by feinting with an action that forces a vulnerable position (reaction). A new player to the sport should keep an open mind.

There are many variants of combinations but in keeping with the theme of this book, we will focus a cluster of three:

- *Ippon Seoi Nage* into *Ko Uchi Gari* (Minor Inner Reap)
- *Uchi Gari* into *Uchi Mata*
- *Uchi Mata* into *Sumigaeshi* (Corner Throw)

Ippon Seoi Nage into Ko Uchi Gari (Minor Inner Reaping)

The first combination introduces a throw not previously covered in this book - *Ko Uchi Gari*. In developing this combination of techniques, it is sensible to take a closer look at Ko Uchi Gari as a single throw in the first instance.

Ko Uchi Gari was at its most effective in the days before the abolition of leg grabs when you could change your grip from the lapel to the leg whilst retaining a sleeve grip. In modern Judo, great care must be taken not to let your free hand slip down to the opponent's leg resulting in either a void throw or possibly a disqualification.

The first example of Ko Uchi Gari demonstrates a rather upright posture with your left hand on the lapel and your right hand on the sleeve. On moving into your opponent, push their left leg forward with your left leg. To execute this version effectively requires great speed, timing and coordination between hand and foot as you need to pull sharply with your right hand to break your opponent's balance sufficiently to throw them.

[41] Assume the standard left-handed sleeve lapel grip in the first instance.

[42] When your opponent steps forward, hook their left foot before they put their full weight down.

[43] Pull sharply with your right hand whilst driving your left arm across your opponent's chest.

Oddly enough, to make Ko Uchi Gari work 'in combination' is somewhat easier than in isolation. The initial opening attack is Ippon Seoi Nage (already covered in our first cluster of throws). Here the emphasis is very much on direction (i.e. turning into the throw as the opponent walks onto you). When contemplating this combination, it is necessary to create a reaction in your opponent. By turning into an upright player not coming forward, their response should be to stand firm and lurch a little backward.

[44] Once again, commence with a standard left-hand sleeve lapel grip.

[45] Stepping into your opponent, you can either drive your right arm upward or grab the top of your opponent's shoulder.

Once you have turned your back on your opponent, step behind your opponent's right leg with your right leg and fall into your opponent's body sliding your right leg to the ground. At the same time, ensure that your right hand continues to grip their right sleeve (there can be a tendency to let go and grab a leg so beware).

[46] In driving your right leg behind your opponent's right leg, try not to land on your knee. As you drive downwards, it is vital to keep hold of the right sleeve with both hands.

[47] The throw is completed by effectively landing on your opponent.

O Uchi Gari into Uchi Mata

There could be a case for describing the second throw in the sequence as *Ko Uchi Gake* rather than Gari. A Gari is a sweep whereas a Gake can be described as a hook or a block. This technique could also be described as Ko Uchi Gake Mata Makikomi (Minor Inner Hook Thigh Winding Throw) In essence, whatever the throw is described as, it is an effective follow up to a failed *Ippon Seoi Nage*. It is effective simply because, as you attack with the first throw, your opponent's reaction should be to lurch backward so they will already be heading in the desired direction. Ensure your knee does not impact on the mat by turning your right leg as you step into the side; this enables the bottom portion of the leg to impact simultaneously.

The second combination in this cluster of O Uchi Gari to Uchi Mata also depends on action/reaction. Using the left-handed grip, this attack can be mounted as earlier described in this book.

[48] Although we have demonstrated the lower lapel grip, if the intention is to throw with Uchi Mata, a higher left-handed grip is desirable.

[49] Instead of driving out with a straight left arm, keep your opponent close by pulling them toward you.

The reaction of the opponent is likely (although not exclusively) to lean forward in an attempt to ensure the leg being attacked - in this case the right one - remains firmly on the ground. This should open up the possibility of the attacker hopping in a backward direction toward the opponent on their standing leg (the attacker's right leg) whilst keeping the left leg in place.

[50] Hop in a clockwise manner into the opponent's body.

[51] Pull sharply with your right arm to force your opponent onto their back.

Uchi Mata (Inner Thigh) into Sumigaeshi (Corner Throw)

The final combination in this cluster is a set that I used to win the Commonwealth Gold medal in Glasgow in 2014 in the -66k final. An unusual combination, Uchi Mata into Sumigaeshi is a venture into the concept of the sacrificial throw.

Any throw where you compromise the standing position for one where you throw yourself backwards onto the mat is described as a sacrificial throw and they are not without their risks. There is always a possibility the throw may not score and your opponent may be able to gain a groundwork advantage and obtain a hold down. In general, and there are conflicting views, sacrificial throws unless well and truly mastered are not throws the novice should be attempting in the early days. A counter argument is a player has to start at some point! However, many top players will complete a highly successful career without one in the armoury. If there can be a safe sacrificial throw *Sumigaeshi* ticks most of the boxes as the thrower casts the opponent's body as far as possible away from their own.

The entry for Uchi Mata has already been described earlier in this book. The attacking left leg simply moves from attacking the opponent's right leg to hooking their left leg just behind the knee [52].

[52] Assuming our now traditional left-handed grip, resist turning in too deeply as with a normal Uchi Mata entry.

[53] Economy of movement is essential so move your left leg across to threaten your opponent's right leg and place your foot just behind their knee.

At this point, sit down whilst pulling hard with your left hand, which should be holding the opponent's right lapel. Once on the floor roll into your opponent to affect a pin if the score has not already scored enough points to win the contest.

[54] Turn your opponent in an anti-clockwise direction using their jacket as you would a steering wheel.

[55] Once your opponent lands, you should continue rolling towards them to secure a hold down if necessary.

There are a number of different forms of Sumigaeshi; this is one variation of them.

In keeping with all the previous clusters, the theme is to minimise movements to assist learning. Yet again, the left hand remains on the opponent's right lapel throughout and it is possible to drill the first two combinations in the cluster without throwing, and only executing the third throw to a conclusion. As such, it is possible to perform technique drills repetitively without your partner constantly having to get up from the mat which can, in itself, be quite taxing.

All three combinations in this cluster are tailor-made for the left-handed grip player to deal with a typical right-handed player even though all the picture demonstrations are with a left on left grip. Indeed, they are as effective on a left on left grip. Always remember that these techniques, as with the previous throws in earlier clusters, are much more difficult to perform on an unwilling opponent.

Cluster Five

The final cluster of throws will demonstrate the fine line between how throws are described. The Judo syllabus consists of many throws, far more than covered in this book, and a newcomer to the sport could be forgiven for looking at a grading syllabus and believing they have lots to study. In reality, the differences are minute and often it seems if a technique is performed badly it carries a different name.

There are four techniques in this cluster, all of which highlight the fine line between how a throw is described.

O Goshi (Hip Throw) and Uki Goshi (Floating Hip)

We have already covered O Goshi, where a player turns their hips completely into a player, however with Uki Goshi (Floating Hip) you only drive one hip into the opponent's body.

[56] In O Goshi your back is flush against your opponent's body.

[57] Uki Goshi is a half turn only, more of a side on attack.

Clearly, there is more chance of throwing a player with O Goshi because when turning your hips into a player, far more control is gained. However, it is often

53

the case that you are subsequently incapable of effecting a complete turn. Half way may just be enough though. The question here is, would any player truly have only a half turn in mind? Probably not, but the half turn gives rise to Uki Goshi.

The next techniques demonstrate what happens when a player overstretches for a throw.

Tai O Toshi and Seoi O Toshi (Shoulder Drop)

Tai O Toshi has already been covered in this book; with Seoi O Toshi (Shoulder Drop) the player stretches a little too far and collapses their knee. This secondary technique might be a throw to specialise in, given that many players have a great deal of success with drop knee throws. This drop knee throw is much gentler on the knee than many others, so is indeed a good one to practice.

[58] A standard Tai O Toshi.

[59] Once the knee collapses, the Tai O Toshi becomes Seoi O Toshi.

The throws, above, are a great basis for developing Judo and building an armoury of throws. Linking them together in clusters it should help to remember them.

An insight into groundwork

An introduction into groundwork (*Newaza*) does not seem to be as regimented as the teaching of standing Judo (*Tachi Waza*). From a standing position, Judo players learn grips, breakfalls, breaking of balance, and that seems (quite correctly) to be the standard format. However, for many years, we have found ourselves at a loss at competition time when we see contestant after contestant start a contest in standing mode (and looking good) but then hit the ground and their minds simply go blank.

Of course, it is not so easy to teach an ideal position on the ground - especially with grips - because you cannot predict how you arrive on the ground in the first place!

A newcomer must learn, in the first instance, how not to lose on the ground. Therefore, the defensive posture is a must.

[60] The classic defensive posture with feet spread to prevent being turned onto your back.

[61] Your arms must be held to your body to prevent armlocks and your chin tucked into your chest to prevent a strangle.

Even juniors not often threatened with armbars or strangles should learn to tuck arms in and protect the neck. Accepting that this is the standard method of defending on the ground it follows that we should study methods to attack an opponent who assumes this posture. The question being... how do you even grip someone who is face down and giving little away?

The first piece of advice is to straddle anyone who hits the deck in a contest *[62]* as it will cause a degree of panic and, more to the point, it will prevent them getting up. Sitting on top of an opponent is a great way of draining energy but may also be a good way of running down the clock in a contest.

If you are leading by a small score then there is little chance of you being pinned if your opponent is underneath you. If they cannot get up then there is no possibility they will be able to throw you. It is a little like a football team leading 1-0 in stoppage time and taking the ball into the corner... horrible to watch (maybe even lacking in sportsmanship) but if winning is everything then a vital tool.

[62] From this position, the player on top is in control and able to plan their next move.

From this position, there are a number of options and, provided your opponent is flat, there is little likelihood of them gaining any advantage on you. Nonetheless, for a referee to allow the newaza to continue it must be seen to be progressive. Here is where we should try to develop a favourite grip. It is probable that your opponent will not wish to untuck their arms from the defensive posture but it is recommended that you should always try to force your arm up through your opponent's armpit and aim to grab their wrist and pin it to their chest *[63]* and *[64]*. This will not be easy but it does mean that when you hit the ground, you have some idea as to where you want to be and, if you are successful, you are likely to panic your opponent.

[63] In clasping the wrist in this manner your opponent will feel threatened.

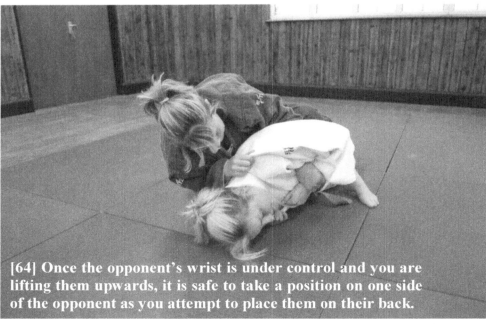

[64] Once the opponent's wrist is under control and you are lifting them upwards, it is safe to take a position on one side of the opponent as you attempt to place them on their back.

The options from here are many, and most would lead to an armlock of one variety or another. However, it may be easiest to turn your opponent onto their back by shuffling around their head - lifting and retaining your grip on your opponent's wrist - and then flattening down and grabbing the belt on the opposite side of the held wrist.

[65] In moving your body above your opponent's head, it should be possible to force their wrist down to the mat.

[66] Whilst retaining the wrist, quickly move your free arm over the opponent's shoulder and affect a hold down.

When practising techniques in Judo, cooperation between partners is vital and players will often be thrown and turned over without resistance. Remember that as you learn a technique - it is not so easy to perform in a contest situation when your opponent is actually fighting back!

It is probably necessary to learn some turnovers that rarely work. The more common turnovers are taught in Judo classes throughout the world and, as such, it is likely your opponent is aware of what you are attempting when you hit the ground. The reason they rarely work is because most Judo players are unlikely to make the errors required to be caught. In knowing the basics, you too will have the knowledge to prevent them.

The double arm roll often taught as a first turnover, requires your opponent to hit the ground and stay on all fours ignoring defensive posture advice.

[67] By driving your arm under the opponent's chin, and clasping their furthest elbow, you secure the head area.

[68] Drive your free arm under the opponent's stomach and clasp the furthest elbow - linking both your hands on the elbow. Pull whilst pushing from your knees with your body.

Had your opponent flattened immediately upon hitting the deck it would have made it difficult to thread your arms under their body to grab hold of the furthest elbows. So, it is vital to learn the turn simply to ensure *you* do not get caught with it. There are many more turns that require your opponent to be inexperienced enough to be turned if they remain on all fours. The message is clear. Do not stay on all fours if you find yourself on the ground in a contest!

The second turnover we cover here is on a similar theme to the first one. You attack a player who has gone flat and it involves attacking through an armpit. In our first turn, it was necessary to straddle your opponent to reduce the possibility of getting your arm trapped underneath their body and being rolled over yourself. It also prevented our opponent getting off the ground. In the second turn it is vital that our bodyweight, through our chest and head, is kept on top of the opponent to prevent them getting off the floor.

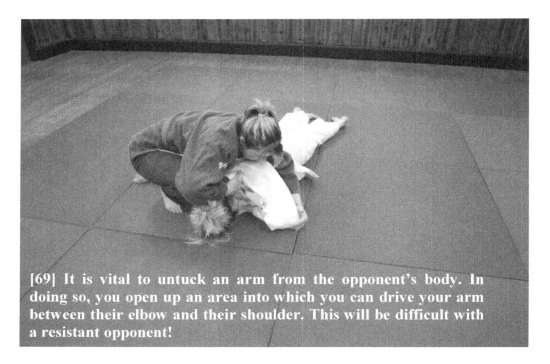

[69] It is vital to untuck an arm from the opponent's body. In doing so, you open up an area into which you can drive your arm between their elbow and their shoulder. This will be difficult with a resistant opponent!

From here, push your opponent's arm out to enable you to thread your arm through the armpit and grab your own lapel.

[70] Although, ideally, you should aim at grabbing your own left lapel the turnover will very likely work if you just take a chunk of their jacket.

Push their opposite arm into their body with your free arm

[71] The left arm controlling the opponent's right arm is vital to succeeding with this turnover.

You should now aim at reaching a position on the other side of their body. To achieve this, shuffle on your knees anti-clockwise around the opponent's head. At no time should you take your bodyweight off the opponent otherwise they will attempt to escape to a standing position. Once your knees are in front of the opponent's head *[72]* you should drive up their shoulder whilst pushing their right elbow into their body. If you fail to control their right elbow, the turnover can be prevented by your opponent reaching out and resisting by pushing down on the mat with their free arm.

[72] At this point of your shuffle around the head, drive your right arm upwards (i.e. knees just above your opponent's head).

[73] The turnover is complete. As long as you keep your opponent on their back, and prevent your opponent from catching one of your legs (with one of theirs) you are in a winning position.

The third turnover is very simple. Again, the armpit is the focus of attack.

If you are facing an opponent who has just dropped in front of you, put your head and chest on top of their back to keep them on the floor and drive your arm under their armpit with a view to placing your knuckles on their neck or holding the inside of the neck of their jacket.

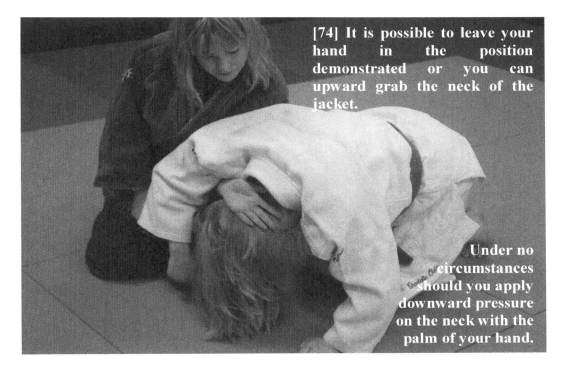

[74] It is possible to leave your hand in the position demonstrated or you can upward grab the neck of the jacket.

Under no circumstances should you apply downward pressure on the neck with the palm of your hand.

Then shuffle, on your knees, around the head in the opposite direction to where your knuckles are placed. Your opponent should roll onto their back. Remember not to place the palm of your hand on the opponent's neck as this could be construed as applying pressure to the neck which is rightly forbidden in Judo. However, with the hand facing upward there is no danger to the opponent's neck or any possibility of being able to apply pressure to the neck area.

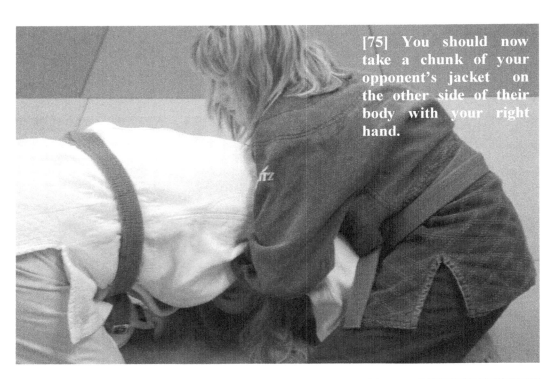

[75] You should now take a chunk of your opponent's jacket on the other side of their body with your right hand.

[76] Moving anti-clockwise around the opponent's body it should be possible to turn an unsuspecting opponent onto their back.

The fourth and final turnover is simply a variation of the third one. Yet again thread your left arm as you did above *[74]*, and then grab a chunk of your opponent's left lapel with the opposite hand.

[77] Assume the same grips as in the previous turnover.

Instead of shuffling to the opponent's left side, the turn is executed by tucking your head into the right side of their body and simply rolling into them.

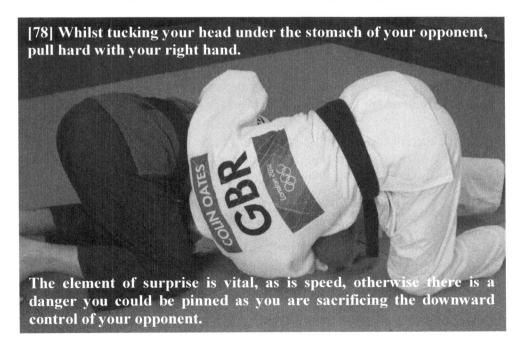

[78] Whilst tucking your head under the stomach of your opponent, pull hard with your right hand.

The element of surprise is vital, as is speed, otherwise there is a danger you could be pinned as you are sacrificing the downward control of your opponent.

Making sure not to lose either of your grips, the opponent should roll onto their back and into a pin down.

[79] The grips employed in turning your opponent over should be strong enough to keep control but keep your chin on their chest at all times. Even if you need to move your grips - you will still be in a strong position.

Both turnovers are linked by the hand threading onto the opponent's neck but the attacking player now has access to a turnover in either direction. Always a bonus in Judo!

So, there are four turnovers with the same theme of attacking the opponent's armpit area. There are many others.

Now we will turn to the reason why we teach turnovers, which is to achieve *Osaekomi* (Hold Down) the point in a contest when the clock starts ticking down to victory (or defeat if you find yourself in the hold down).

Just like throwing (tachi waza) it is possible to teach a pattern of hold downs. Traditional katas, whilst very educational, require an uncomfortable and not very attractive approach to newaza with tori performing an awkward one legged crawl before reaching uke. Logistics of space also prevent this style of teaching in the majority of dojos.

The method known as 'around the clock' - a system by which a player circles the opponent lying flat and performs a series of hold downs moving from one to another - is ideal for teaching a variety of hold downs. There are many ways in which you can move fluently from one position to another but the prime objective here is simply to teach a variety of hold downs. The fluid movement of one to another will come with practise.

The hold downs covered are

1 *Kesa gatame* (Scarf hold)

2 *Kazure kesa gatame* (Broken scarf hold)

3 *Kami shiho gatame* (Upper four quarters hold)

4 *Ushiro kesa gatame* (Reverse scarf hold)

5 *Yoko shiho gatame* (Side four quarters hold)

6 *Mune gatame* (Chest hold)

7 *Kazure tate shiho gatame* (Broken lengthwise four quarters hold)

8 *Kata gatame* (Shoulder hold)

9 *Kesa gatame* (Scarf hold)

Whichever around the clock system is adopted, and there are many, they all seem to start and finish with *kesa gatame [80]* which is the ultimate in hold downs. Escaping from this hold is very difficult and escape often depends on luck.

[80] This hold down can be performed with a variety grips; the principle one being control of one arm and the neck.

Let us first look at the individual hold downs that should be covered in our around the clock system.

There are varying bodies of opinion as to whether you should keep your head to the ground. Only by actively fighting opponents on the ground will you be able to appreciate the wide variations. The intention is to control an opponent on the ground for a duration of time such that you win the contest. If that means lifting your head up, or placing it further on the ground, to buy more seconds on the clock it matters not where your head or even your grips are.

[81] This form of Kesa Gatame demonstrates a lowering of the head; it is permissible to place your chin on the opponent's forehead too (though the latter is somewhat less friendly).

The next hold down moves to *kazure kesa gatame* (Broken Scarf Hold).

[82] Removing your hand from around the opponent's neck is often required if your opponent attempts to bridge out from the hold down. Your free hand is there to act as a support to prevent you being rolled over.

As can be seen, the attacker has been taught two separate hold downs simply by removing the arm circling the neck, and placing it firmly to the right of uke's head.

The third hold down in the circle is *kami shiho gatame*.

[83] From this position it is very difficult for your opponent... all of your body weight is above their head making any form of bridge or lift unlikely.

The hold demonstrated shows tori's arms underneath uke's shoulders. In newaza, or a contest, this is not so easy to achieve but the principle of the hold down is to make sure your head and chest is over the head and chest of your opponent. You then have control of the left and right hand sides of their body, the bottom line being to keep them there for 20 seconds or so.

Continuing to move in a clockwise direction the next hold down to slip into would be *Ushiro Kesa Gatame*.

[84] As with the previous hold, you effectively have all your bodyweight over the head making a successful escape difficult. If you are unable to secure the belt, any part of the jacket in that area will suffice.

Next in the movement is *Yoko Shiho Gatame*.

[85] There is an option to grab the tail of the opponent's jacket rather than the leg.

From this position, the attacker can straddle the opponent and pin their right arm with the attacker's head for *Kazure Tate Shiho Gatame*.

[86] A particularly effective hold down as you can neutralise your opponent's arm with your head. Your right hand should grip the jacket behind your opponent's neck.

Keep the opponent's right arm pinned to their head (using your head) and move over their body into *Kata Gatame*.

[87] Again, your head will render one of your opponent's arms immobile and free your left arm.

Finally, release the opponent's arm to revert back to *Kesa Gatame*.

[88] Back to where you started with a hold down on the other side of your opponent. The round the clock format is complete.

This method of tuition teaches variety of hold downs and gives both student and coach a structure to work with. Of course moving around a resistant opponent is very much a different proposition.

Is there any way out of a hold down?

The short answer is yes. However if you find yourself in a contest and hear the referee say *osaekomi* (the hold is on and, in a contest, the clock is ticking down to the time required to win) then you are in big trouble. Under present day rules, it is only necessary to hold an opponent down for 20 seconds to win a contest. If you are fortunate enough to have thrown your opponent for *Wazari* (7 point rated throw) the time is reduced to 15 seconds. Either way there is very little time to get away.

Many a player, over the years, may have attended clubs where they have heard a coach explain how it is possible to twist away from various holds. The coach will tell of countless escape moves but the bottom line is that most hold downs can only be escaped from if you are physically strong and certainly stronger and heavier than the person on top of you. There are many in the sport who would say that Judo is all about technique, and size and strength are not factors. Most who make this statement are generally six foot plus and weigh 100kg or more. The truth is that size and strength *are* factors, which is why Judo tournaments have different weight categories to level the playing field.

Despite the above being true, as a novice player you will need to learn the principle of escape. Oddly enough, it is possible to prepare student players to learn the basic principle in a warm up with bridging exercises.

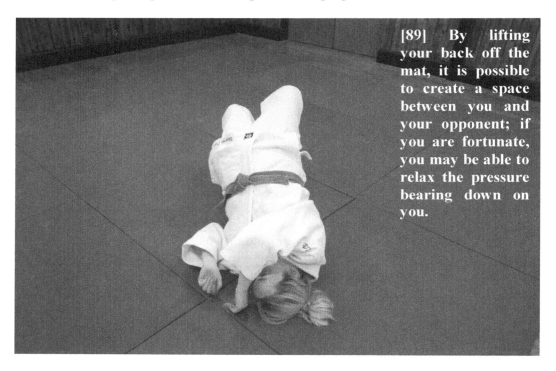

[89] By lifting your back off the mat, it is possible to create a space between you and your opponent; if you are fortunate, you may be able to relax the pressure bearing down on you.

[90] Bridging onto either shoulder is a great exercise as well as vital in groundwork situations.

The idea is to create a space between you and the person pinning you to the mat.

[91] A standard kesa gatame hold down with the head high (it would be tougher to perform the turn out if the head is low to the mat) and your opponent is in command.

[92] By bridging away from your opponent and pushing hard with your trapped left arm, the space provided by the bridge may enable sufficient leverage to begin a turnout from the hold down.

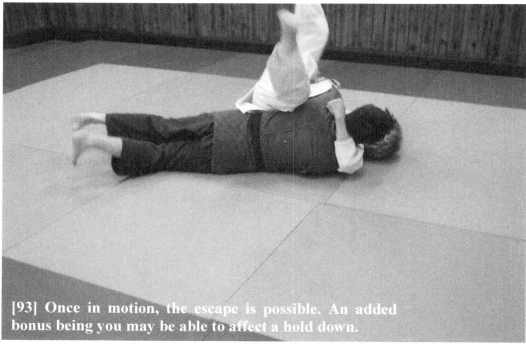

[93] Once in motion, the escape is possible. An added bonus being you may be able to affect a hold down.

It is just possible you may create sufficient space to turn into your opponent. You must aim to place your free arm between you and your opponent. The intention is turn onto your front and eventually pull your trapped left arm from your opponent's clasp.

[94] By bridging and turning the opposite way and into your opponent's body, the aim is to place your free arm between your head and that of your opponent.

[95] If your opponent is too strong to turn across your body, as in the previous escape, try to trick your opponent by turning the other way.

[96] In bringing your knees up, and in placing your free arm between you and your opponent's body, pull hard with your trapped left arm; if successful it may just be possible to escape.

In reality, if you have lost a firm Kesa Gatame hold down, the person underneath would have achieved escape through 90 % strength and 10% technique. The hold down of Kesa Gatame is a very difficult hold to escape. It is more likely you will stop the clock by intertwining your legs with one of the legs of your attacker.

[97] Although the opponent is still on their back, the clock is not ticking down. Very often this the best option to avoid defeat.

Whilst this stops the clock, it does not create an escape as you are still underneath your attacker, and not in good place. It is up to the discretion of the referee as to when a hold can be broken up. While you are in that compromised position, there remains the possibility that your attacker will free their intertwined leg and set the clock ticking to defeat again.

The only other escape we will cover is in relation to *yoko shiho gatame* as it involves a different principle to bridging 'upwards and out'.

If you are being pinned with yoko shiho gatame, aim to push your opponent's head towards your leg by placing your arm under their chin.

[98] A firm hold of the Judo jacket is required and by placing your elbow into the opponent's neck and pushing hard, you will find it possible to guide their head towards your right leg.

Remember, in Judo it is illegal to place a hand on the face of your opponent. Under the chin is allowed.

If you are fortunate enough to push the head far enough down, and you are relatively flexible, it just might be possible to bring your leg up far enough to replace your hand with your leg *[99]* and hence sit up and break free of the hold down.

[99] At this stage, by placing your leg where your arm had previously been the hold down is already seriously compromised.

[100] Your opponent's head has nowhere to go and by sitting up you will be in a position to turn the tables on your opponent.

[101] You are now in a dominant posture and able to effect a hold down yourself.

The crucial thing is to remember that all escapes must be performed within 20 seconds to avoid defeat, and within 10 seconds to avoid conceding a score.

Hold Down Times
10-14 seconds | YUKO | 5 point score
15-19 seconds | WAZARI | 7 point score (if already a 7 point score down, the contest now ends)
20 seconds | IPPON | 10 point score; end of contest

It is often said that if you practise groundwork and standing work for say one hour each a week your groundwork will improve at twice the rate. It is certainly true that groundwork appears to be more physically draining. It is not unusual to see a disparity in size and weight of players in groundwork - possibly because the risk of injury is less. In standing practice, there is always the risk the bigger player may land on you with unpleasant consequences. Obviously all players are unique, and many of the bigger players (male or female) will almost certainly act in a responsible manner in standing randori; nonetheless, there are greater risks of accidents when bigger players are matched with their smaller counterparts and newcomers to Judo should remain conscious of this at all times.

At this point, let's look at survival techniques when engaging in newaza with bigger, stronger, or simply more experienced players.

Always remember that if you find yourself in distress - simply tap your opponent at least twice. Under the rules of Judo in the dojo, your opponent will let go. At higher levels, players have sometimes been known to be cynical and deny they have tapped out after you have let them go in good faith. Hence, in a contest, let the referee call Ippon and matte before you completely give up your advantage.

Of course, tapping out in newaza is not much of a survival technique! But if you are confronted by an immoveable object (of which there are many in Judo) at least you live to fight another day.

The defensive postures from earlier in the book *[60]* and *[61]* show how to fend off defeat and make life difficult for a superior newaza specialist. In a contest, it may just buy sufficient time to force the referee to stand up the contest. As such, try to avoid only flattening out in practice. Instead, try rolling onto your back and placing a scissors with your legs around your opponent's waist. In this position, you are relatively safe and able to work (underneath) on potential strangles or armlocks.

[102] In a scissors manoeuvre, you are not allowed to squeeze your opponent's trunk but this will allow you to work from underneath a stronger opponent and force them to (somehow) get beyond your legs. This is not easy... even for the more experienced player.

It also helps if, from underneath, you cross grip by digging your wrist as deep into your opponent's neck as possible, driving your hand deep into their lapel. This will make the aggressor, on top, conscious that their neck is at risk of attack.

[103] By digging your thumb into the jacket, the bone part of the wrist will quickly feel uncomfortable against the neck.

If you are lucky and the attacker forces their head low enough, place your free arm around their neck then grab your arm and squeeze. The attacker might just be the one tapping out.

[104] If possible, place your free left arm on the other side of the opponent's neck and grab your sleeve and squeeze.

[105] A strong opponent may be capable of simply picking you off the mat. In these circumstances, a referee will halt proceedings regardless of whether the strangle is taking effect. It is a form of escape from any groundwork position.

This book is not intended to cover strangles or arm locks in any depth, but it is worth noting that many of the best opportunities to apply these techniques will come from underneath an opponent. The obvious drawback is that if your opponent is strong enough to lift you off the mat in a contest) the referee will call matte and stand you up. As such, a great deal of skill is required here.

The final piece of advice for groundwork practice or instruction, for any novice, is *never* surrender your upright posture. This is a bit like saying 'never get thrown' but the moment you concede your posture - you are in trouble. Often, an experienced player will deliberately collapse onto all fours and lower their head simply to allow a novice to work on their turnovers. A newer player should avoid doing this if possible as it will invite attack after attack and prove physically draining. Most groundwork practice in a dojo starts from the somewhat fake scenario of facing your opponent on all fours *[106]* and *[107]*. If your head is forced down, you are fighting a rear-guard action.

[106] The somewhat false way in which groundwork commences in a dojo; although most groundwork competitions will start with one knee on the mat only.

[107] The more traditional way groundwork commences with both knees on the mat.

Some clubs try to introduce some realism into newaza by orchestrating a throw and going straight into newaza and this is a tried and tested formula that clearly helps. To assist transition, randori can performed under contest rules, which means that players can follow down after throwing someone. This requires a high level of coach vigilance on the mat and limits the number of players that can do randori at any one time so is perhaps not suitable for all dojos.

The great thing with groundwork is that age has little relevance and it is possible to take up the sport late in life and become highly proficient. With standing, on the other hand, you are always likely to be a half second slower than the younger player if you take up the sport later in life.

An insight into strangles, chokes and armlocks

It may seem strange to separate strangles, chokes and armlocks as most of these techniques will be performed on the ground. There are a number of *standing* strangles and armlocks but, in reality, they are rarely applied with any degree of success.

To the beginner, this side of Judo must seem somewhat barbaric especially since

Judo is our gentle art. Obviously, there is very little that is gentle in applying an armlock or strangle!

This section is intended to cover the principles of this side of Judo. Let's start with some definitions.

What is a strangle? A strangle can be described as applied pressure to the carotid arteries in the neck of the opponent.

What is a choke? A choke can be described as applied pressure to the opponent's windpipe.

What is an armlock? An armlock can be described as applied pressure to the elbow joint.

The above techniques are designed to make your opponent tap out, causing the referee to stop the competition. None of these techniques should be applied in a jerky movements, rather, they should be applied progressively otherwise serious injury or lack of consciousness may occur.

The majority of books tend to describe strangles and chokes with the person applying them underneath their opponent. Whilst this is possible, it is very likely your opponent will try to escape by lifting your body off the mat which (in a contest) leads to the referee calling a halt to the movement. To make any of these techniques work it is vital that you have control of your opponent's body and this is where being able to keep your bodyweight on top of your opponent is of paramount importance.

Before describing a basic strangle it should be pointed out that whilst there are a multitude of strangles (all with different Japanese names many of which are quite difficult to remember) the difference between strangles can be as simple as having a thumb inside the collar versus outside the collar. In short, the effect is very much the same. At the end of the day if you gain a submission victory in a contest it does not matter which side of the collar your thumb ends up.

A basic strangle: Namijujime (Normal Cross Strangle)

This strangle cuts off the blood supply to the brain by blocking the carotid arteries at the side of the neck and requires a crossed hands grip and thumb placement on the inside of the collar *[108]*. You then turn your wrists into your opponent's neck.

There are conflicting views as to whether this works better if you straddle your opponent and lean over them (leaving your wrists where they are) or whether you should pull down on your arms. Either way, control of your opponent's body is vital.

Experimentation with strangles is vital but ALWAYS under the supervision of an experienced coach as they can be dangerous. With this particular strangle the opponent can easily pass out so care must be taken.

[108] By placing your thumbs on the inside of the jacket, you should turn your wrists into your opponent's neck to exert pressure.

It is doubtful whether your opponent will ever be caught by this strangle whilst standing. with their arms be by their side. They will be trying to push your arms away.

A basic choke: Hadaka Jime (Naked Strangle)

Hadaka Jime is a simple technique that applies pressure to the windpipe and which, if applied properly, will attract a very speedy submission.

It is often described as being applied from behind someone's back. This is, of course, a very unlikely scenario as few players would present their back to you in this manner. However, it does nicely show the hand and arm positions. It is most likely to work if you straddle an opponent and are able to thread your arm through your opponent. Hence the reason for teaching the defensive posture earlier in this book to prevent just such a situation.

[109] Clasp your hands together and gently squeeze until your opponent taps. This strangle does not require any grip of the opponent's jacket.

Again, experimentation will be required to make this work effectively. Usually, you should try to get the bony part of your wrist as deep into the neck as possible.

A basic armlock: Juji Gatame (Cross Arm Lock)

Any pressure applied to an elbow joint is likely to induce a prompt submission and there are many differently named armlocks. But, like strangles and chokes, they are mostly variations on a theme. The armlock entitled *juji gatame* conjures up a vision of what your objective should be in no uncertain terms. The only way this can be demonstrated is with an uke who is flat on their back.

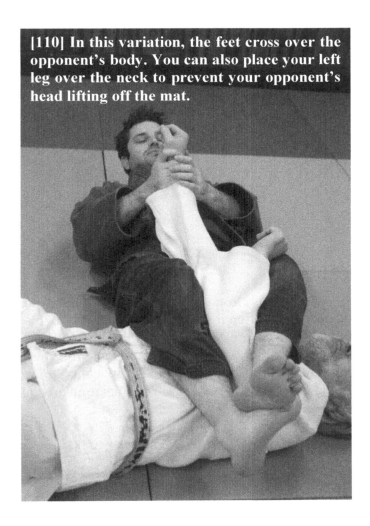

[110] In this variation, the feet cross over the opponent's body. You can also place your left leg over the neck to prevent your opponent's head lifting off the mat.

[111] Another view demonstrates the position of your opponent's arm.

Make sure your backside is as close to uke's body as possible and that their thumb is pointing upwards. Often it will be necessary to lift one's hips to force the submission. Many players are amazingly flexible and can resist for long periods in Judo contests especially where there are major medals at stake. When practising at club, remember that the continuous application of armlocks in a session will result in members of your class having particularly achy elbow joints in the morning!

Always remember to apply with progressive pressure and to release when uke indicates/taps.

The three techniques in this section do not just 'present themselves' in either a newaza session or a Judo contest. Various turns have been devised to roll opponents into armlocks and strangles and these can be found in a more specialised publication. In the same way that not all throws are guaranteed to work for you neither will all turns lead to a strangle or armlock.

Concluding Remarks

This book is intended to guide a beginner into the sport of Judo or enhance a player's knowledge through a different approach to Judo instruction. Many individuals have studied from a book before walking onto a Judo mat but, obviously, a book is insufficient to make you a master Judo athlete.

Unlike sports where you compete against a clock or a distance, in Judo you are trying to defeat another thinking person. Yes, it is true, you can do lots of gym work to build up body strength or increase turning speeds by training against a stopwatch but in Judo it is only through practice with players of varying sizes, experience levels, and particular specialisms that can you truly develop.

There are many families with one or more Judoka. There are probably many more with sofas that have been battered into submission by brothers or sisters throwing each other across the living room and onto a soft surface. The best place to practice Judo is at a club with a qualified instructor and a set of Judo mats. Indeed under no circumstances should arm locks or strangles be practiced outside a Judo club – *they are dangerous*. Many of the throwing drills within this book can be practiced at home with a willing partner as many of the clusters have been designed to be user friendly in not completing the throws. Your partner can for the most part remain standing.

The issue of finding a club can be problematic in itself. The first port of call is the British Judo Association and they will be able to furnish you with a list of clubs with qualified coaches

Once you have found a club you should find out who the coach is, whether he has a history in coaching or as a player. A bit of internet research can go a long way.

The first night at a Judo club can be a little daunting but give the club a chance and try not to pass judgement on the first couple of visits. If it turns out that the style of coaching or theme of the club (some clubs are competitive and some more gentle) is not for you – do not give up straightaway. Give another club a chance, many a player has walked away from the sport without realising that clubs and coaches are different and there is one out there that is probably right for them.

Of course, it may be that your local Judo club is not a member of a governing body. This need not be an issue as there are many non-affiliated Judo clubs in the world that are for one reason or another not affiliated to their nation's governing body. Many such coaches are very capable and operate independently for their own reasons. The one area that should not be compromised, however, is in making sure that these clubs carry reliable insurance and the coach is qualified and reputable. Only by attending or observing such sessions can any final assessment be made of their quality. It is vital that you obtain a Judo licence as quickly as possible as with most licences (again check out the detail before making a commitment) insurance is included which covers you against any claim against you for injury. It is extremely rare that any incident will ever occur that leads to a claim but in the modern world it is not a risk worth taking. In any event, you will need a licence to grade or compete at any level in a competition.

When looking for a judo club also check out the venue and the mats being used. Judo mats should be about 40mm thick, if they are less thick, player safety could be compromised. Indeed 40mm mats on a concrete floor can be somewhat problematic for heavyweight players. There may also be not so obvious dangers around the mat area like heating radiators that are not covered. Carefully look at the mats themselves, their general condition and whether there are gaps between them because of corner damage (all mats tend to move and create gaps but mats with damage should be removed from service). A player or parent can learn much about a club just by checking out its equipment and location.

When attending a Judo club please remove jewellery and remember that hygiene is of paramount importance. Finger nails and toe nails should be clean and short. Whatever clothing you may be wearing (whether sweat shirt or Judo suit) should be clean. Judo is a full contact sport and nothing is worse than having to perform drills with a partner who has not made the effort before walking onto a Judo mat.

Finally, remember that Judo is a subject for study and no matter how long you practice, you will eventually experience something that seems like a mountain to climb. If you took up piano lessons, you would not expect to play a concert in a few weeks. There would be hour upon hour of practice to master that 'tricky bit' that always catches you out. Eventually, given time you will master that piece of music though. Judo is no different. Hours of practice will lead to improvement. Climbing that mountain is achievable, just do not give up.

ENJOY YOUR JUDO!

Tipping The Balance: The Mental Skills Handbook For Athletes [Sport Psychology Series] by Dr Martin Turner and Dr Jamie Barker

At the highest level, athletes are highly skilled, highly trained, and highly proficient machines. Take the 100m sprint for example. All of the athletes in the Olympic final can run sub-ten seconds. They are all fast! But on the day, the deciding factor is often not how fast they are, but rather, how fast they can run under the high pressure circumstances of an Olympic final. The ability to deal with pressure is not about any physical or technical skill, but is more about what goes on between the ears – in other words, it is psychological and about performing with freedom, dealing with distractions, regulating emotions, maintaining self-confidence, and trusting the body's ability to deliver under pressure.

Tipping The Balance offers contemporary evidence-based and highly practical mental strategies that help an athlete to develop the crucial mental skills that enable them to thrive under pressure, perform consistently when it matters most, and enjoy the challenge of the big event.

This book is about empowering you - the athlete - no matter what level you perform at. In this book you will discover the secrets of how the world's greatest athletes draw on cutting edge psychological skills to use what's between their ears to maximize performance.

Published 1 November 2014| ISBN: 978-1-909125-93-3| 284 pages | £14.99 | Print, Kindle and iBooks

The 7 Master Moves of Success by Jag Shoker

One of the most common clichés about success - that it is a journey, not a destination - has concealed one if its most defining qualities. Success really is a dynamic and ever-moving process. It is about making the right moves at the right time.

In this absorbing and uplifting book, Jag Shoker – a leading performance coach to business leaders, sports professionals and creative performers – brings the science and inspiration behind success to life. He reveals the 7 Master Moves that combine to create the high performance state that he calls Inspired Movement: the ability to perform an optimal series of moves to create the success you desire most.

Drawing widely on scientific research, his extensive consultancy experiences, and insights into the successes of top performers in business, sport, and entertainment, *7 Master Moves* is a synthesis of the leading-edge thinking, and paradigms, that underpin personal performance and potential. Building upon key research in fields such as neuroscience, psychology, expert performance and talent development - *7 Master Moves* represents an evidence-based 'meta' theory of what really works. Compelling to read, and easy to follow, the book incorporates a strong practical element and shares a number of powerful and practical exercises that can help you apply each Master Move and achieve greater results in your life and work. Regardless of your profession or passion in life, the 7 Master Moves will reward those who are prepared to work hard to achieve the success that matters most to them.

Published 6 June 2014| ISBN: 978-1-909125-59-9 | 228 pages | £9.99 | Print, Kindle and iBooks

The Way Forward: Solutions to England's Football Failings
by Matthew Whitehouse

English football is in a state of crisis. It has been almost 50 years since England made the final of a major championship and the national sides, at all levels, continue to disappoint and underperform. Yet no-one appears to know how to improve the situation.

In his acclaimed book, The Way Forward, football coach Matthew Whitehouse examines the causes of English football's decline and offers a number of areas where change and improvement need to be implemented immediately.

With a keen focus and passion for youth development and improved coaching he explains that no single fix can overcome current difficulties and that a multi-pronged strategy is needed. If we wish to improve the standards of players in England then we must address the issues in schools, the grassroots, and academies, as well as looking at the constraints of the Premier League and English FA.

Published: July 10 2013 | ISBN: 978-1909125193 | 236 pages | £12.99 | Print, Kindle and iBooks

Lightning Source UK Ltd.
Milton Keynes UK
UKOW07f0311151115

262715UK00001B/10/P